a little book of love

Rachel Clifton

BookLeaf
Publishing

India | USA | UK

Presentation by *BookLeaf Publishing*

Web: www.bookleafpub.com

E-mail: info@bookleafpub.com

ISBN: 978-93-5744-495-8

First edition 2022

DEDICATION

for aa~

your love brings me to tears
in the best possible way.

thank you for being my friend.

ACKNOWLEDGEMENT

I wouldn't be me without you.

without everything I've experienced and been
through,
and all the wonderful people I've met along the
way.

proudly, resolutely
insatiable.

with gritted teeth, and tears in my eyes—
my life is only just beginning.

onward.

I love every inch of you.

PREFACE

caught in the struggle between who I am
and who I want to be
but who I am is who I want to be.

*this is the journey
and the reward, too.*

I don't have to know you to love you.

we are already whole.
we are already worthy.
we are already home.

first come, first served

avalanche
brainwave
an exploration of softness
wholeness
abundance
freedom

dance with me, darling
dance with me

I wanted my first poem to be beautiful
and so, it is
and so, we are

healing
leaving
feeling
lifted
lifted
lifted

HIGHER

call me ascendant
watch me rise

phoenix
shapeshifter
graceless
horizons

there is no room for scarcity
for not-enoughness
for too-muchness
but darling, there is room for you
and all of me

let us rest our weary bodies
let us rest in peace.

if not now, then when?

I will make time for myself
[even] when my heart aches
I will love myself
[even] when I am in pain

I will be fierce and raw and unapologetic
[even] when I am afraid

I am,
I will,
transcend

this body is a conduit
this life, a mirror
life, lust,
from dusk to dark
I am here
and I am listening

all that's left is surrender.

grounding

grounding
the descent into being
of the body, embodied
flesh-skin-tingling

playing with language and
sensuality
the essence of the known
a deeper understanding of the world
a cry to be heard

my body is my temple
without it, I cannot stand tall
without it, I cannot stand at all
we make curious bedfellows

and there's something about that bleary-eyed
place
between sleep and woke
between night and day
that makes me want to stay
soften
surrender
to the afterglow

we are already beautiful—
we are enough as we are.

god is a woman

I am learning how not to hide
from myself, first and foremost.

this is a little book of love.

lines blur. I don't know if this is a journal entry
or a poem, but I'm rolling with it.
rolling with the punches. riding with the tides.

She sings to me.

She sings to me and reminds me of who I am
when I doubt myself.

this unnamed She is a mystery,
but who or what She is
is secondary to
what She gives me and how She makes me feel.

alive. inspired. humbled. grateful.

punctuation is
underrated, but I'm
over this bullshit

God is a woman.

wax lyrical

wax lyrical
on vulnerability:
feeling, healing, being
softly—
this life is a motherfucking journey
[so]
take it slow.

taste it. taste me.

savour every moment between
chipped front teeth and molars
tongue it, ravish it
let it take you places you've never been

let yourself truly *see*—
and be seen.

this is an ode to greatness
and an ode to love—
a love of, and within
a deeper flame
ascending
a trusting, a knowing, a holding

space for everything

so you can look up to the heavens and remember
THIS IS WHAT IT MEANS TO BE ALIVE

from my heart to yours,
I wish you love—
and, for what it's worth

there is no exit.

interlude

I missed a day.

I was busy living
doing something different
and I hate the word
'obligation'

just spitballing on a page

~ ~ ~

you have a gift

when you speak
simply, and from the heart
you move mountains

and so,
I get out of my own way.

chronicles of narnia

you told me you liked fantasy
or rather, you showed me
and, for what it's worth
I wanted to be your[s]—
unedited
formless
graceless
but we can't pick and choose

only the dogs will save us
I hear 'em howling
keen eyes and slavish jaws all slobber
wolfy, effervescent
all I ever wanted was companionship
[I think]
well, we certainly got it
it's just you, me, and the hounds, baby
domesticated bliss

p.s. I stole your wardrobe

take your aim

I don't know
how to
describe myself
but I know how to limit myself

ashes to ashes
moth to flame

I write because
it connects me with my soul

that's all this is:
Home.

ricochet

everything i know about love

expansion at a level of being

dare
to
dream

what would it mean to
soften

your
power
is
sovereign

the first cut is the deepest

we all want it

I thought I 'knew'
but I was wrong

it doesn't have to hurt.

a little act of love

it was a little act of love
to write this
and to share

I let myself dissolve
just a little—
I let myself be tender

there is something heartfelt about
putting pen to paper

the elegant disarray

moving past fear and shame
to FEEL—
just to feel
and to express

it says
(I say)
I'M HERE
I'M NOT LEAVING YOU
I'M HERE TO STAY

for it was a little act of love simply to listen and
my life is peppered with
such small things—pleasures, moments,
memories

unimaginable peace
unimaginable hope
unimaginable dreams

the carcass of the child I never was
embraced, and laid to rest

honoured, mourned, replenished

THIS IS REDEMPTION—
we [can] always [have] love.

ekphrasis

call me by my name
ART

exposed, beautiful, sublime
let me tell you one thing—
I want more than wanting to be wanted

women and desire.

i'm not satisfied with crumbs anymore

I'm not satisfied with crumbs anymore.

I see through it, you, me
actions are nothing without intention
and words are nothing without action
but it's not that your love isn't enough—
your love is more than enough.

you are more than enough, I am more than
enough
we are enough, abundant, whole
just as we are, I promise—

it's that I want more
from this, with you

FROM LIFE

than you want or
can give.

both can be true
both can be right
both can be freeing

I like the shape these words make
on the page, the ripple of
space and undulation, CURVES

it's kind of sexy. it kind of turns me on
but shh—this is a poetry book

(I'm not satisfied with crumbs anymore)

carnal

I had to include something sexy
or I'd be doing myself
an injustice

this poem is
NSFW and
fuckable

because I
just couldn't resist

tell me what makes you
wet, depraved, and horrified

I'll show you what makes you
powerful

expansion

where are you
fulfilled?

what makes you feel
warm?

how do you
take care of
every inch of your beautiful self?

and what makes you feel
cared for?

these are the questions we should be asking
ourselves

me? I'm a conduit

nothing more
and
nothing less

I'm here to learn
and I'm here to love

nothing else
matters

pearls of wisdom

shaken, not stirred
fall-out, afterglow, grappling with something
intangible:
(S)He who shall not be named

the bittersweet pangs
of longing, of feeling, of
being full and in my body
and FLESH, not just bones
and whole
SO WHOLE
no lack
no hole
JUST JOY

I felt loved with you
I feel loved without you

and here is something undeniable:
the stories we tell ourselves are so fucking
powerful

creatrix

the best things
are unexpected

there is nothing to seek
we are already home

(I never want to force these words)

it hurts to soften
but that pain is a gift, too

these words bring me to my knees and make me
feel deep
Devotion

so here I am
sharing a little piece of my heart
with you

queen

every time I betray myself
I also betray everyone I love
because I don't let them love
me for me

I don't let myself be seen
I don't let myself be known
I don't let myself be honoured
I don't let myself be worshipped

but most of all
I don't let myself be
a motherfucking queen
(sexuality is fluid)

no more——
onward.

radical softness

I want to be
radically soft—
you know, that feeling of
release / give me / more

I want to be the kind of woman who
feels and is felt

wild grace, kinda imperious, fucking medieval
a freak in the bedroom

I want to be MY OWN
and I am

and I am
home

I'm inspired by a love that doesn't waver.
I'm inspired by uprooting my own shame.
I'm inspired by the process of unravelling.

I'm inspired by the way
we change.

every time I see that smile on your face

it brings me to tears

yes, I'm fucking soft—
so be it

I wouldn't have it any other way.

what is my truth? - part 1

I am in service
to what is timeless

I may be afraid
but I am willing

I may be fearful
but I am not impeded by it

I exist on a wave of
Love
and protection

this too
is timeless

I do not have to understand
to trust
to love
to open

I do not have to
have or be
anything more than

who and what
I am

darling,
all we are is welcome

~~~

when I take care of myself first
I take care of everyone else
better

I teach myself to be compassionate
and stretch the limits of my generosity

I let myself move
and be moved
with snake-hipped curiosity

and, most importantly,
I let myself be

everything else takes care of itself.
~~~

what is my truth? -
part 2

I see my shadows

I feel my yearnings

I know my shame
intimately, desolately

I feel my isolation
and I let it take me—

I let it save me
again and again and again

~~~

these words are a tidal wave
as above, and so below

I AM NOT FEARLESS—
I am *feeling*

that is enough
that is everything
~~~

~~~

I want to be
really
fucking
soft

to break myself open
and feel
and live
and love

deeply and unflinchingly

I want to emanate
Love
from every pore

and I am, I am, I am

I DO

and I do just by being

~~~

thank you for teaching me
that home was always [in] you

we love each other
in the way/s we know how [to]

I admire your bravery.

baby

birthing something
new and beautiful and precious—

you are mine, and yet
wholeheartedly, unapologetically
your own

and I love you for that,
I love everything you stand for

I love how you move me
need me
derail me—
how weak you make me feel
and how you are changing me

and most of all,
I love how I am changing

cradled in
all your innocence,
you grant me
peace

we are already perfect

we are already free

thank you for letting me
live

~~~

and when I take care of myself,
I learn to love

as a child might
as a child does

and so, I soften
and so, I open
it's never too late

[we all have needy little inner children]

darling,
let me hold you.
~~~

prophecy

these words are a prophecy.

I think, therefore I am
or will be—
a light ringing in my ears
tinnitus? or
grace Becoming me

I see Divinity in all things
as much love as pain as fear as freedom as
COSMIC RELEASE

the stillness of
letting go

the heart and soul of
DESIRE AND HUNGER AND
FLESH AND FREEDOM
rippling as we
weave our magic
in and out
stirring, seething, persisting
DARING TO ASK FOR MORE
and give more to
the golden bucket

the infinite chasm
of LIFE itself—
liberation in motion

LIFE
my love, my light
and my greatest teacher

you bring me to tears with your wisdom
and teach me how to soar

what you see in me is what I see in you

and to me, you are
perfect beyond words

thank you for the music
these songs are limitless

I've never felt as much joy
as I do in your arms.

www.ingramcontent.com/pod-product-compliance
Lightning Source LLC
LaVergne TN
LVHW010919200726

843509LV00013B/1990